Using Ten Frames
to Teach Number Sense

Carson-Dellosa Publishing LLC
Greensboro, North Carolina

Credits
Copy Editor: Julie B. Killian
Layout and Cover Design: Nick Greenwood

Carson-Dellosa Publishing LLC
PO Box 35665
Greensboro, NC 27425 USA
www.carsondellosa.com

ISBN 978-1-60996-471-9
05-167141151

Table of Contents

Introduction 4

Using the Mats. 6

Whole-Class and Small-Group Lessons and Games

    "One, Two, Buckle My Shoe" 8

    Show Me 9

    Roll Again. 10

    Estimation Station 11

    More Than, Less Than 12

    Fishing for Numbers 13

    Match Me 14

    How Many Number Sentences Can You Find? 15

    Drop 10. 15

    Fastest to 20 (Fastest to 0). 16

Five-Frame Mats. 17

Ten-Frame Mats 27

Double Ten-Frame Mats. 55

Introduction

Introducing the Ten Frame

A ten frame is simply a model that helps students develop a visual understanding of the numbers 1 to 10. A ten frame develops students' "subitizing" skills, or the ability to see "how many." These concrete mental images result in more flexible strategies to use for mental math. The ten frame becomes the tool students use as they move from the concrete to the pictorial to the abstract in their understanding of numbers.

The ten frame helps with the following skills:

- Counting

- One-to-one correspondence

- Part-whole relationships

- Number relationships

- Basic facts

- Place value

- Regrouping

A ten frame uses the numbers 5 and 10 to develop these skills. By using ten frames, students can easily see the parts of numbers. In the example shown, students can see that 8 is 3 more than 5. They can also see that 8 is 4 and 4.

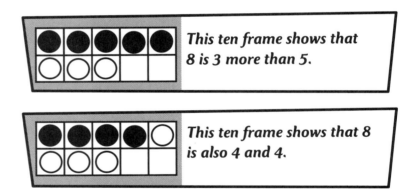

This ten frame shows that 8 is 3 more than 5.

This ten frame shows that 8 is also 4 and 4.

When using ten frames, direct students to place their frames horizontally and have them place counters in the boxes, starting with the top-left box. Have students fill the spaces across the top row before moving to the bottom row. Tell students that they should also fill the bottom row from left to right. Below are examples of ten frames filled with the numbers 1 to 10.

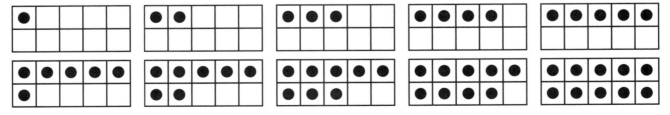

Introducing the Double Ten Frame

When first introducing ten frames to students, focus instruction on numbers less than 10 in terms of their relationships with 10. This will help build a strong foundation of basic addition and subtraction facts for 10, which is extremely important for higher-level math concepts and mental calculation. However, once students master initial concepts, use a double ten frame to help students further develop their understanding of place value, regrouping, and basic facts to 20.

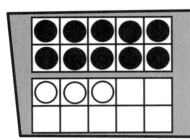

*This double ten frame shows that **13 is 10 and 3**.*

*(This double ten frame also explores place value by showing that **13 is one ten and three ones**.)*

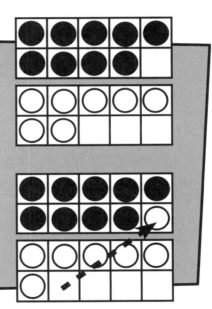

This double ten frame shows 9 and 7. To determine the total number of counters, students use strategies that help them develop mental calculation skills.

To add the counters, students learn that they should make a ten first and then add the remainder. This double ten frame now shows 10 and 6. Students deduce that if 10 and 6 is 16, then 9 and 7 is 16.

CD-104535 • © Carson-Dellosa

Using the Mats

Provided in this book are 24 mats: 5 five-frame, 14 ten-frame, and 5 double ten-frame. Each mat has a particular theme or character that is perfect for developing language along with number sense. Prepare the mats ahead of time by laminating them and then cutting off the counters at the bottom of each mat. Store the counters in resealable plastic bags. Then, place each mat and bag of counters in a large envelope or pocket folder and place at a math center. You may also reproduce the mats for any of the lessons in the book or keep them at the center for students to explore part-whole relationships as they hone their basic math fact knowledge.

The engaging art on each mat is perfect for connecting literacy and math. Below are some suggested children's books to use with the selected mats.

Mat: "Tutus and Ballet Shoes," page 21
Shoes, Shoes, Shoes by Ann Morris (HarperCollins, 1998)

Mat: "Goldfish Friends," page 45
Fish Eyes: A Book You Can Count On by Lois Ehlert (Sandpiper, 1992)

Mat: "Sitting Pretty," page 25
Five Green and Speckled Frogs by Priscilla Burris (Cartwheel, 2003)
Turtle Splash: Countdown at the Pond by Cathryn Falwell (Greenwillow Books, 2008)

Mat: "From Seeds to Sunflowers," page 55
In My Garden by Ward Schumaker (Chronicle Books, 2000)

Mat: "Jelly Jars," page 49
Mr. Cookie Baker by Monica Wellington (Dutton Juvenile, 2006)

The mats can also inspire both you and your students to create short poems to use while learning number concepts. Following are examples of poems created for some of the mats in this book. The blank lines in the poems indicate where numbers should go as you recite the poems.

Mat: "Parrots in Puddles," page 19

Drip, drop, plink, plonk,

The rain does fall.

But _____ parading parrots

Aren't bothered at all.

Splashing through the puddles

In boots and hats,

_____ parrots join the fun.

How many is that?

Mat: "Best in Baseball," page 35

I have _____ baseball cards

In my special book.

Come get closer

And take a good look!

Add _____ new ones

Just given to me.

Now how many cards

Do you see?

Mat: "Tutus and Ballet Shoes," page 21

Little bears dance

In pink tutus.

_____ stop dancing

To tie their shoes.

The teacher says,

"Oh how can this be?"

Now how many dancing bears

Can you still see?

Mat: "What's for Lunch?" page 37

The clock on the wall

Says, "It's time for lunch!"

_____ little fish go out

In a bunch.

Still hard at work,

Some fish we find.

How many now were

Left behind?

Mat: "Beads of Fun," page 23

Let's have fun

And string some beads.

Put on one

We have just begun!

String _____ more

To make it long.

One to start

And now we have _____!

Mat: "Starry Nighttime Sky," page 59

Tick, tock, tick, tock,

Say, "Good night"

_____ shiny stars

Bring the twilight.

In the night sky,

_____ more I see.

How many shiny stars

Will this be?

7

Whole-Class and Small-Group Lessons and Games

"One, Two, Buckle My Shoe"

Whole-Class Lesson

Skills: counting to 10, number and number word recognition

Materials: ten frames and counters (one set per student), nursery rhyme

1. Begin the lesson by displaying this nursery rhyme. Have students say it several times until all of the students can say it fluently.

2. Distribute the ten frames and the counters. Tell students that a ten frame is a tool that will help them keep track of the numbers in the rhyme.

3. Recite the rhyme slowly. Have each student place a counter on the ten frame to show each number.

"One, two, buckle my shoe."

4. Continue reciting the rhyme. Have each student place a counter on the ten frame as he says each number.

5. The poem ends with the phrase "start over again!" This becomes the prompt for student practice.

6. Give students independent practice time. Observe students to informally assess their progress.

CD-104535 • © Carson-Dellosa

Show Me

Whole-Class Lesson

Skills: counting to 10, number and number word recognition

Materials: pocket chart, sentence strips, ten-frame mats and counters (one set per student)

1. Place a sentence strip with the words *Show Me* in the top pocket of the pocket chart.

2. Program a sentence strip with a number or a number word and place it under the words *Show Me*.

3. Ask students to build that number on their ten-frame mats. Emphasize one-to-one correspondence between the number and the counters on the ten frame.

4. Display a ten frame with the correct number of dots.

5. Ask students to check their models. Assist students who may need help checking or correcting their models. Students can also help check each other's models by asking, "Do our models look the same?"

6. Have students continue to build and check numbers. Observe students to informally assess their progress.

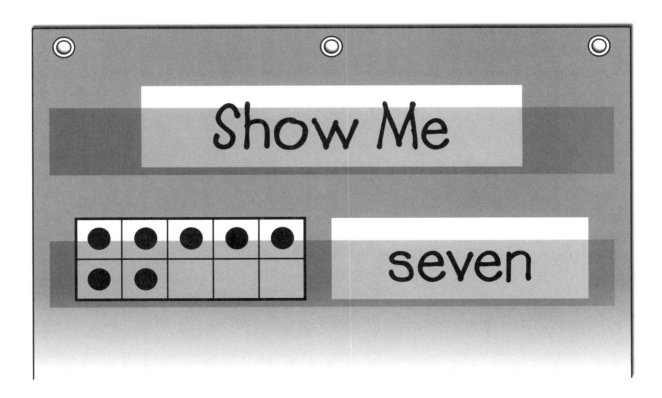

Roll Again

Small-Group Game

Skill: comparing numbers

Materials: ten-frame mats and counters, dice

1. Distribute ten-frame mats, counters, and one die to each pair of students. Place the counters in a pile in the middle of the game-playing area.

2. Have each player roll the die. If the players roll the same number, have them roll again.

3. Have each player put the matching number of counters on her ten-frame mat to represent the number on the die.

4. Have the player with the greater number take a counter from the pile.

5. Have each player clear her ten-frame mat and roll the die again. Play continues until the pile of counters in the middle is gone.

6. For a variation, after players compare their numbers, reward the player with the lesser number a counter.

CD-104535 • © Carson-Dellosa

Estimation Station

Small-Group Game

Skills: estimating, counting

Materials: ten-frame mats, container of small manipulatives (buttons, beans, chips), tally sheet to record points

1. Have one student reach into the container, pull out a handful of manipulatives, and place them on a table.

2. Have the other player or players estimate how many the student pulled out of the container. Then, have them build their estimated numbers on their ten-frame mats.

3. Have the student who pulled out the manipulatives use them as counters on his ten-frame mat to confirm the amount.

4. The player with the best estimate gets one point. Now, it is her turn to pull out a handful of manipulatives.

5. Have her return all of the manipulatives to the container. Play continues in a repeated manner until one player has a determined number of points. For example, the player with 5, 8, or 10 points wins.

More Than, Less Than

Small-Group Game

Skills: comparing numbers, subtraction, addition

Materials: two decks of number cards with the numbers 1 to 10, ten-frame mats and counters, tokens or manipulatives for rewards

1. Have a player shuffle each deck of number cards and place the decks facedown in stacks.

2. Tell each player to select a card from the deck and place it faceup on the table.

3. Have each player use her ten-frame mat and counters to build the number she has selected from the deck.

4. Direct players to use their ten-frame models to compare the number each one has built.

5. The player with the greater number wins the token reward. Before she can collect the reward, have her explain her thinking. For example, if the cards selected were 5 and 3, the player with the 5 card should say, "Five is two more than three. I get two tokens."

6. Have players continue until all of the cards have been used. The player with the most tokens wins the game.

7. For a variation, after players have compared their numbers, award the player with the lesser number a token once she has explained her thinking.

Fishing for Numbers

Small-Group Game

Skills: finding sums and differences for 5, 10, 15, or 20

Materials: two sets of number cards, paper for recording answers (optional)

1. Shuffle both sets of number cards together and give each player five cards.

2. Place the remaining cards number-side down in the center of a table.

3. Have players look at their cards to see if they can pair them to make sums for 10 (or 5, 15, or 20). If they have any pairs for these sums, have players lay the pairs of cards in front of them.

4. Once all of the players have established the sums they were dealt, it is time to "fish" for numbers.

5. Have each player continue to try to make sums for 10 (or 5, 15, or 20) by asking other players for a number card. For example, "Kevin, do you have a two?"

6. If the asked player does not have the requested number, he should tell the other player to, "Fish for the number."

7. That player will draw a card from the deck.

8. Players continue to fish for numbers and make equations with their cards and check and/or record their answers.

9. The player with the most pairs at the end of the game wins.

10. For a variation, have players use two-color counters and ten-frame mats to show the pair of numbers and the sum.

Match Me

Whole-Class Game

Skill: identifying numbers

Materials: set of ten-frame mats with dot patterns 1 to 10, set of number cards programmed with the numbers 1 to 10, string, hole punch, scissors

1. Assemble ten-frame and number-card "necklaces" by punching holes in the upper corners of the ten-frame mats and the number cards. Tie string through each hole to create a necklace.

2. Distribute the necklaces to students. Have students place the necklaces over their heads with the ten frames or numbers facing their bodies. When you say, "Match up," students should flip their necklaces around.

3. Next, tell students to find the player who has the same number (the ten frame or the number) on his necklace. Once a player finds the correct match, the pair should sit until all player pairs are matched. (Note: You can play a song or time players while they search for their matches.) Monitor the pairs of players for correct matches.

4. Have players return their necklaces to a pile and distribute them again to repeat the activity.

CD-104535 • © Carson-Dellosa

How Many Number Sentences Can You Find?

Center Activity

Skill: identifying parts and wholes

Materials: set of number cards programmed with the numbers 1 to 10 (or 1 to 20), two-color counters, ten-frame mats, sheets of paper

1. Have each student choose a number card and build that number on a ten-frame (or double ten-frame) mat. Tell students to begin with only one color of the counters showing.

2. Instruct students to record on the sheets of paper the number sentences they see on their mats. For example, if a student built the number 7 with red counters, she would write $7 + 0 = 7$.

3. Students should continue to record as many number sentences as they can for the number chosen. Have them do so by flipping over one counter at a time to the yellow side. The two colors now represent the two addends in the number sentence. The sum will always be the same.

Drop 10

Center Activity

Skill: identifying facts for 10

Materials: ten-frame mat, 10 two-color counters, sheet of paper

1. Show students how to hold the 10 counters in their hands and drop them carefully onto the ten-frame mat. Instruct students to move the counters to the ten frame and record the number sentence indicated by the colors of counters. For example, if 3 landed with red faceup, and 7 landed with yellow faceup, students would record $3 + 7 = 10$.

2. Have students continue to drop counters and record number sentences until they find all 11 facts for 10 or until it is time to move on to the next center task.

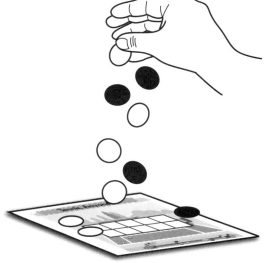

Fastest to 20 (Fastest to 0)

Small-Group Game

Skill: counting on and counting back

Materials: double ten-frame mats, number cube (faces programmed with the numbers 1, 2, and 3), counters

1. Place a pile of counters in the middle of the students. Have a student roll the number cube and take that number of counters from the pile and place them on his double ten frame.

2. Instruct him to pass the number cube to the next student. Play continues until one student fills her entire double ten frame first.

3. For a variation, have students start with 20 counters each on their double ten-frame mats. As each student rolls the number cube, have him remove that number of counters from his mat. Play continues until one student has reached 0.

CD-104535 • © Carson-Dellosa

Pencil Power

cut

CD-104535

Beads of Fun

✂ cut

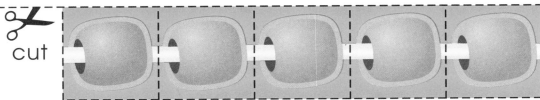

CD-104535

Sitting Pretty

cut

Friends in Frames

© Carson-Dellosa

✂ cut

Tennis, Anyone?

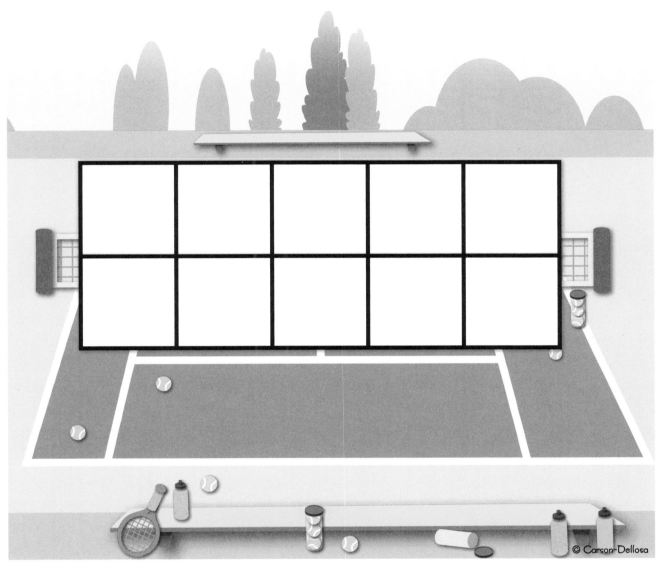

© Carson-Dellosa

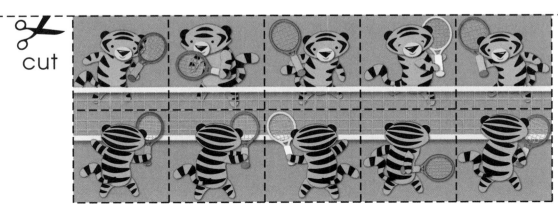

cut

Best in Baseball

© Carson-Dellosa

cut

CD-104535

© Carson-Dellosa

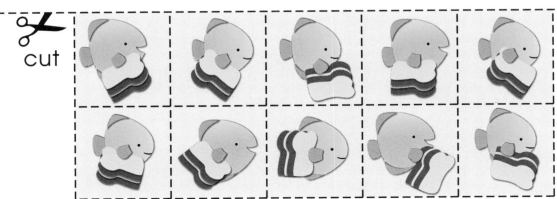

cut

CD-104535

Quilt Squares

✂ cut

Prized Pumpkin Patch

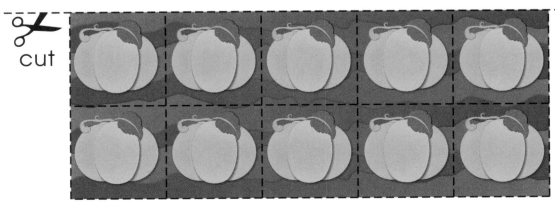

✂ cut

Let's Play!

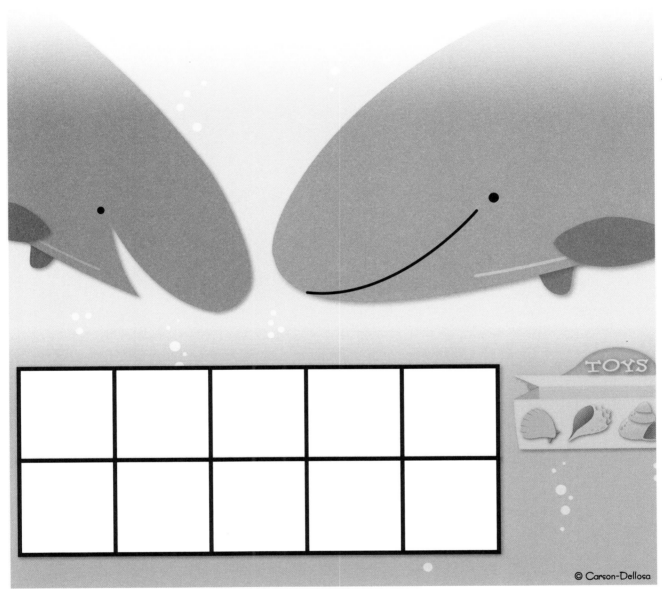

cut

CD-104535

Goldfish Friends

cut

CD-104535

Saving Pennies

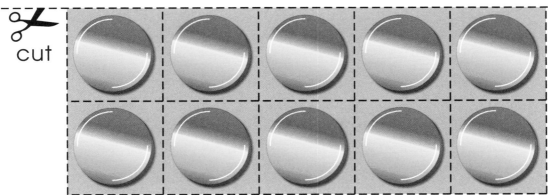

cut

Jelly Jars

© Carson-Dellosa

cut

Going to School

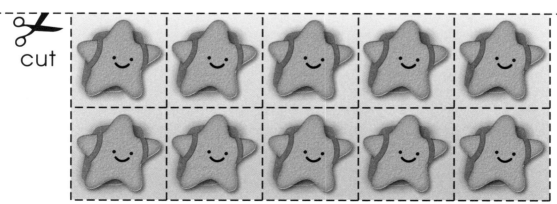

cut

Ladybug Count

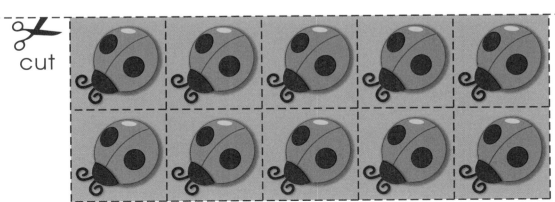

cut

From Seeds to Sunflowers

cut

CD-104535

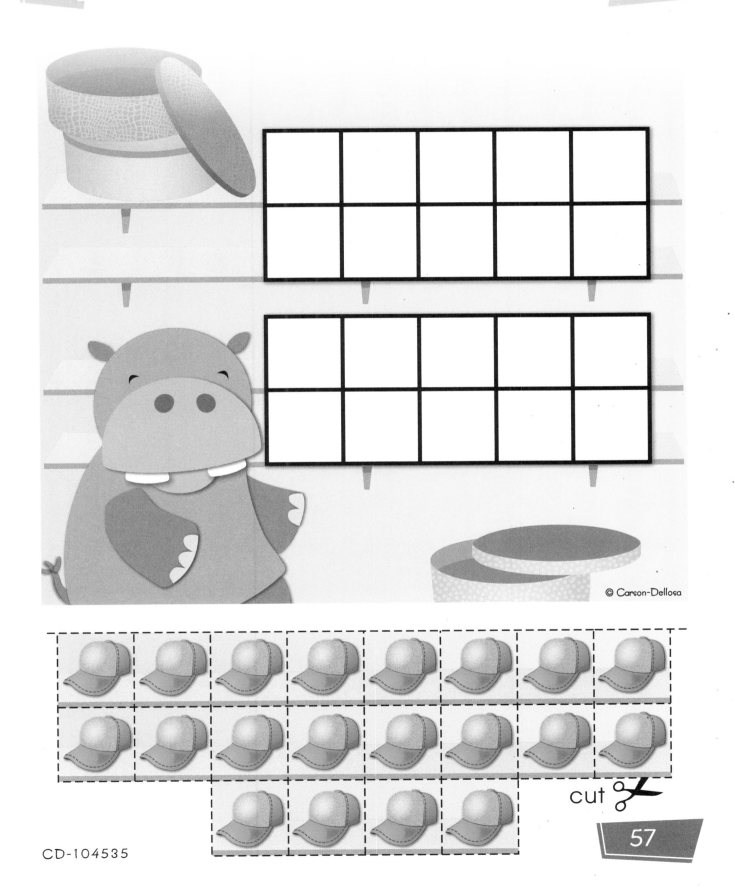

© Carson-Dellosa

cut

CD-104535

Starry Nighttime Sky

cut ✂

CD-104535

Super Sticker Fun

© Carson-Dellosa

cut

CD-104535

Many Matching Marbles

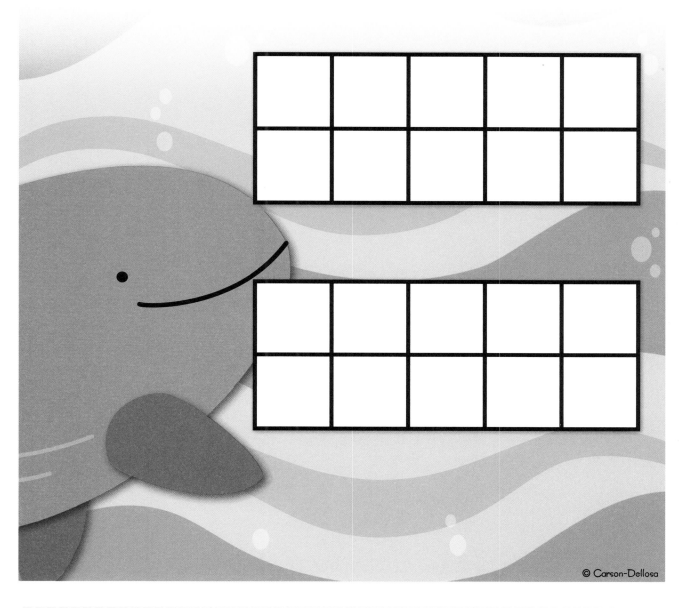

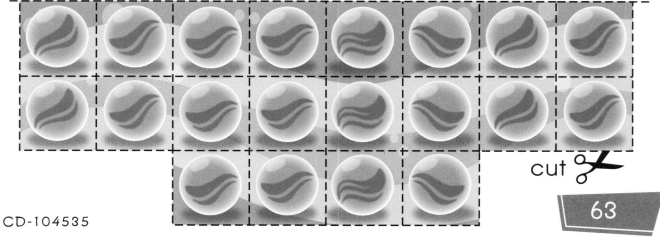

cut

CD-104535